WOOLWICH
REVIEWED

Hog Lane

A grimmer side of life in the Woolwich 'Dusthole' during the 1880s. Hog Lane was a street of great poverty with many low lodging houses where building styles of many centuries were crowded together. It ran parallel to Surgeon Street between the High Street and the river. In 1889 the right-hand side of the road had been knocked into Surgeon Street to form the broad approach to the new Woolwich Free Ferry which was opened by the London County Council (LCC) with considerable ceremony. The ancient cantilevered houses on the left were not demolished until the 1930s.

WOOLWICH REVIEWED

by Julian Watson

with photographs by
Stephen Moreton Prichard

Greenwich Libraries
London Borough of Greenwich
1986

Acknowledgments

Publication of *Woolwich Reviewed* would not have been possible without the interest and support of John Lowry, Borough Librarian and Alex McIntosh, Assistant Director (Arts).

My grateful thanks are due to past and present colleagues at Woodlands: Barbara Ludlow, Veronica Moore, Eileen Hopgood and Len Reilly who have all made considerable contributions to *Woolwich Reviewed.*

I am indebted to Ralph Burnett for his valuable help with the captions to the photographs, which have benefitted enormously from his immense knowledge of Woolwich and its history.

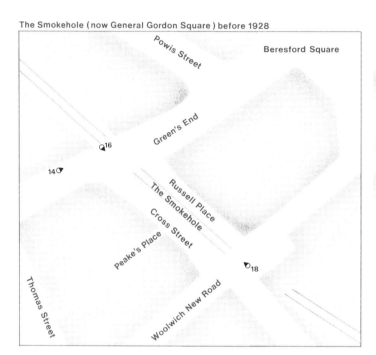

The Smokehole (now General Gordon Square) before 1928

Design by Kit Gregory
Photography by Stephen Moreton Prichard
Edited by Wendy Gregory
Typeset by Blackheath Photoset
Printed by Berryman & Sons Ltd.

Contents

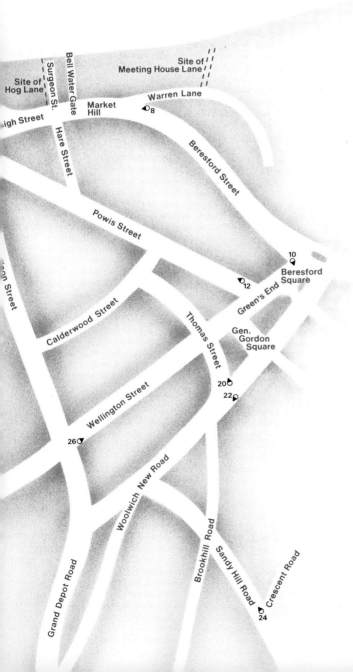

page
2 Hog Lane
6 Preface
8 Market Hill
10 Beresford Square
12 Powis Street
14 Green's End
16 General Gordon Square looking south
18 General Gordon Square looking north
20 Thomas Street
22 Woolwich New Road
24 Sandy Hill Road
26 Wellington Street
28 Woodrow
30 Woolwich from the river
32 Woolwich Ferry

Cover photograph

A remarkable photograph of the junction of Meeting House Lane and Woolwich High Street in 1880. William Hatcher's greengrocery shop is on the corner. This stretch of the old High Street is now part of Warren Lane and has changed so drastically as to be unrecognisable today even though the lane still follows the old road's course. The street formed part of the 'Dusthole' – an area of Woolwich where even the police hardly dared to enter. The buildings were completely cleared away when the Woolwich Power Station was built in 1912.

Preface

Historian Ian Nairn's comment on Woolwich, made in 1966, highlights the central theme of the town — that of constant change throughout its history. This metamorphosis is still at work today as Woolwich adjusts from her former rôle of industrial powerhouse, serving Britain's naval and military forces, to a modern commercial centre of hi-tech, light industry and local government administration.

The town has a long history. Built on the site of a Roman settlement on the banks of the River Thames, its Saxon name, *Vuluvic,* is recorded in a charter of 918 AD. The tradition of operating a ferry service across Woolwich Reach can be traced back to at least the fourteenth century. Woolwich first came to prominence in 1512 when King Henry VIII establishd a Royal Dockyard here to build his new flagship the *Great Harry.* The Dockyard prospered for over 350 years before it was finally closed in 1869 along with its neighbour at Deptford.

The foundation of the Dockyard attracted many other industries to Woolwich: England's first salt-glazed stoneware kiln was set up in the early seventeenth century by the site of the south pier of the present-day ferry; a Ropeyard was laid out in 1574 and in 1694 the Royal Laboratory was founded on the Warren by the river to manufacture ammunition, fuses and gunpowder. The Royal Laboratory later spawned the Royal Arsenal — Britain's principal ordnance factory, which reached peak production during World War I when it was the district's major employer. In 1716 the Royal Regiment of Artillery was founded in the Arsenal and this in turn led to the foundation of the Royal Military Academy. In 1776 and 1806 respectively these institutions moved to Woolwich Common where their fine buildings are still to be found.

During the last century Woolwich grew rapidly under the influence of the naval and military establishments within her boundaries. Improved river and road transport and the coming of the railway in 1849 also contributed to the town's development. In the same century some well known Woolwich organisations came into existence: Woolwich Polytechnic (1890), the Royal Arsenal Co-operative Society (1868), Woolwich Equitable Building Society (1847) and Woolwich Arsenal Football Club (1886) which later moved to Highbury and became today's Arsenal FC, or the *Gunners* to their fans. During the first half of the last century an extensive shopping centre was developed on land owned by the local Powis family.

However, these affluent developments contrasted starkly with the great poverty in the old riverside areas of the town. There was, of course, a grimmer side to Woolwich. Some present-day 'Woolwichers' still talk of the 'Dusthole' — a small unlit area of dank riverside behind Beresford Street between the Arsenal Wall and the Ferry. Here misery and squalor reigned. It was an area of dingy lodging houses populated by the destitute and homeless. A district where the poorest local prostitutes plied their trade and which was *officially* out-of-bounds to soldiers. In one typical hostel it is recorded that five families shared one room with only the flimsiest of blanket partitions to preserve their privacy. Now, happily, nothing but memories remain of the deprivations of the Dusthole.

Victorian Woolwich was, despite its seamier side, a popular tourist centre — the visitors being especially attracted by the work at the Arsenal (security demanded that only foreigners needed a pass to enter in those days); and by the comprehensive collection of guns at the Rotunda Museum, the Royal Artillery's Museum of Guns. A tourist guidebook of 1852 talks of 'tens of thousands of visitors' visiting the attractions of Woolwich — and the enlightened are still coming today.

The old photographs in *Woolwich Reviewed* concentrate on 'civilian' Woolwich (military Woolwich would need a separate volume!) and reflect a Woolwich still remembered by many: the one o'clock gun; Sunday Church Parade at the Barracks; the outpouring of thousands of workers from the Arsenal; the sight and emotive smell of the gleaming machinery on the old ferry boats; the 'Smokehole' which

'Thumping self-centred vitality;
complete freedom from the morning train to Town.
It is always being rebuilt,
as it must be — that is its nature.'

vented steam from the trains in the tunnel beneath General Gordon Square; Saturday-night shopping in the Square with its myriad bargains and entertainments. A town full of life and prosperity, a youthful town with many and varied opportunities for well-paid work. And where, after work, leisure time could be enjoyed at the many cinemas and theatres (sadly fewer nowadays); in the pubs; at the swimming baths — in 1902 these were considered the best in London; walking in local parks and woodland; or simply watching vessels from all over the world slip quietly by on the Thames. The quality and reputation of many Woolwich shops was unsurpassed a century ago. Powis Street was dominated by the original Co-op (RACS) and Messrs Garrett's *Gigantic Emporium* was a particularly fashionable and comprehensive store advertised as being 'regularly patronized by all classes'.

The town today is much altered by social and economic change. It is the centre of local government for the London Borough of Greenwich and boasts a thriving shopping centre and market. Many of the features which made Woolwich prosperous in previous centuries are still here, to be seen and admired as they take on new rôles as historic monuments or adapt to more twentieth-century functions. The old switching station for instance has become *The Tramshed,* a busy social centre and home for all types of theatre and musical activities.

The old photographs in this book have been carefully chosen from the large collection at the Local History Library in Blackheath. These views, taken between eighty and a hundred years ago, reveal much of the character of the town at the height of its growth and prosperity.

The present-day photographs have been specially taken from the same viewpoints. Many scenes contain features which are recognisable today and illustrate a pleasing historical continuity; others show parts of Woolwich which have changed so drastically that it is difficult to believe that they depict the same place. Two historic views which appear in the book are unpaired — this is because we feel that their inherent interest justifies their inclusion. The present-day equivalents have been omitted as these sites have changed so radically and, sadly, not for the better, that they contain little of interest even to today's most devoted sightseer! They are Hog Lane (now Old Ferry Approach) and Woolwich High Street (now a part of Warren Lane).

The collection at the Local History Library has been built up largely by the generosity of local people who have donated their photographs for the enjoyment of the whole community and for future generations. In times of such great change it is important that these fragments of our heritage should be preserved and appreciated. We hope that the publication of *Woolwich Reviewed* with its insight into our shared past will encourage and inspire other potential donors to delve into attics, trunks and other dusty hiding places in order to enlarge our collection. Photographs, artifacts and documents will all be gratefully received — if not available on a permanent basis then we will be happy to copy them.

We hope that the book will be of interest to a wide audience — not only to local people and confirmed Woolwichophiles. From the magnificent Thames Barrier — the most ambitious piece of civil engineering in Britain — to the Rotunda — a Regency tent, converted into a permanent building by John Nash in 1822 — there's plenty in Woolwich to interest and amuse visitors and residents alike.

Julian Watson
Woodlands

A part of Woolwich High Street and heart of the old riverside town. The photograph is taken from just below the old market place (Market Head) looking towards the approach to the old free ferry. On the left, dominating the picture, is an impressive display of goods outside Mr Thomas the pawnbroker's shop. Next door, at number 106 in 1922, was Mrs Leach the confectioner. Alfred Skillman, furniture dealer at number 108, provides a direct link with today, his family's name still appearing boldly above the shop. On the right, with a dustcart outside, is the *Crown and Anchor* public house — sadly no longer there. One can speculate that the man with the jug in the foreground was on his way to the *Steam Packet,* another local hostelry.

*By water to Woolwich, and walked back from
Woolwich to Greenwich all alone. Saw a man that
had a cudgell in his hand, and though he told me
that he laboured in the King's Yard, yet, God
forgive me, I did doubt he might knock me on the
head with his club. But I got safe home.*
Samuel Pepys 1662

This pre-First World War postcard shows a busy corner of the market, near the junction with New Road. The customers, who appear to be almost exclusively men, are probably Arsenal workers on their way home. The buildings on the left include the *Ordnance Arms,* managed in 1905 by Alfred Pamment; Endean's Leather and Grindery Merchants at number 17 and the Leading Boot Company at number 16 — both premises occupied by similar businesses today. The market has been in the square officially since 1888 but traders began settling there earlier, having migrated from the old market situated between Market Hill and the river. This part of the market specialised in fish and several stand-pipes were provided for hosing down at the end of the day. The building with the mansard roof in New Road is now Bloomfield's Bakery.

*The essence of Woolwich is Beresford Square. It is
Woolwich bovrilised. At half an hour past noon the
Arsenal gates open upon it, and it becomes the
property of the Amalgamated Society of Engineers.
In the evening it belongs to aimless sauntering
soldiers and their ladies.*
The Outer Circle — Rambles in Remote London Thomas Burke 1921

Powis Street

Powis Street has always been Woolwich's best shopping area. This view from c1925 looks towards the tower of the RACS building in the distance. Pryce's were a long-established Woolwich firm and the biggest printer in the town. Their first floor rooms were used as a school and as the meeting rooms of the Woolwich Scientific Society during the last century. George Carter and Sons, hatters, traded at numbers 37 — 39, and beyond them Wood Bros, the furniture dealers, offered 'easy terms'. On the extreme right are the showrooms of the South Metropolitan Gas Company and further along the street the sign of H Samuel, the jeweller, can be discerned.

*The finest place in the world, full of colour and
excitement, with something new to see every day.*
Homes and Gardens Ruby Ferguson Jan 1967

A pre-First World War postcard of the view towards Beresford Gate from the junction with Russell Place (now General Gordon Square). The sight of thousands of employees pouring out of the Arsenal and through this gate is now only a memory. The gate has lost its link with the Arsenal and has become a feature of an improved Beresford Square. On the left, at number 11 Green's End, is the Home and Colonial Stores, with Stephenson the hatter next door. On the right is Birts and Son where a vast range of household items were for sale, including the 'perfect transposing piano'. The low wall on the immediate right of the photograph conceals the infamous Smokehole.

I love the noise of men. That is why I love Woolwich. It possesses no external beauties, no excellences of line or feature, it is tricked with no fair clothing. To love Woolwich one must love one's kind.

The Outer Circle — Rambles in Remote London Thomas Burke 1921

General Gordon Square looking south

The transformation of this area from the Smokehole to General Gordon Square was a tribute to the campaigning spirit of local traders, particularly Thomas Brown, a tailor of Hope House, 3 Russell Place (the north side of the square). He and his fellow traders were fed up with their goods and shops being coated with soot from the open cutting which ventilated Woolwich Arsenal Station. Mr Brown made a model and drew a representation of how he thought the square ought to look and got up a petition of 20,000 signatures. The opportunity to get rid of the Smokehole came at last when the line was electrified in 1926. The Cross Street side of the square housed a diversity of businesses. Murray's Car Hire and Barron's Ostrich Feather store are on opposite corners of Peake's Place, an ancient alleyway which still exists as a right-of-way across the square.

General Gordon Square looking south

*. . . it seems somehow to have collected the dust and
held the spirit of many centuries.*
London South of the River Sam Price Myers 1949

In 1928 work on filling in the Smokehole was completed and the square was officially opened with much public celebration. The man largely responsible, Thomas Brown, appears in both the old photographs on this page and on page 16. This venerable, and it is said kindly, white-haired man, is seen holding the placard proclaiming 'Gordon Square' on page 16. The whole of Russell Place was redeveloped after Birts, the freeholders, sold out in 1931 and Mr Brown had to move his tailoring business to new premises in Thomas Street. The new Woolwich Equitable building on the right of the modern photograph was opened by Sir Kingsley Wood on 14 May 1935.

*Woolwich seems like some antique army pensioner,
wounded in the wars and cast upon a not
noticeably sympathetic world.*
A View of the Thames Norman Shrapnel 1977

Thomas Street

Thomas Street seen from the junction with New Road before the First World War. The *Fortune of War* beerhouse (on the right) is now a Hindu temple and is adjoined by Montrose House where a Mr W Brown ran a tailor's shop for many years. In those days a Scotch tweed suit could be had for 50/- (£2.50). Opposite, in Green's End, David Davis's upholstery shop can just be seen. On the left-hand side of Thomas Street is Woolwich's Main Post Office — little changed today apart from a single-storey extension which was added in the 1920s. The cart in the foreground, outside the Post Office, belonged to Cox's dairy of Maxey Road.

Woolwich is more than a suburb. It is a provincial town. Peopled by cockneys, it yet stands apart from the Metropolis.
The Outer Circle — Rambles in Remote London Thomas Burke 1921

This scene has hardly changed today apart from the addition of Peggy Middleton House which now fills the right-hand side of the road and replaces the barracks seen in this postcard photograph. New cars now fill the bars of the old *Gun Tavern,* and the Presbyterian Church with its spire, seen beyond St Peter's Catholic Church, has long since disappeared —but most of the buildings have survived. The oil jars high on the wall of number 81 indicate that this was the site of George Mence Smith's Oil and Colour shop.

Woolwich (wu·lidʒ). 1794. The name of a town in Kent, used attrib., esp. to designate productions of its old dockyard and the Royal Arsenal, as *W. gun, hulk; W. infant,* a joc. name for certain heavy guns.

Shorter Oxford English Dictionary

Sandy Hill Road

Looking down Sandy Hill Road from near the *Fort Tavern* — a scene little altered in almost a hundred years, apart from the introduction of the motor car. The terraced houses on the right are Hope Place and at the bottom of the hill, in Brookhill Road, a part of the Cambridge Cottages (the married quarters for the Woolwich Garrison) is just visible. The towers of the Parish Church of St Mary Magdalene, the Presbyterian Church and the Town Hall can be seen clearly. The first building on the left belonged to Howell & Son, antique restorers and upholsterers. The wall in the right foreground concealed the yard of Kinnersley's Bakery in Crescent Road.

Sandy Hill Road

It is one of the few districts in London where the workman has made the side and crests of the steep hills his own.
Life and Labour of the People in London Charles Booth 1902

Wellington Street

Wellington Street in about 1910. *The Star* public house on
the left is still there, although its surroundings have changed
— it now stands near a busy junction with the South Circular
Road. In 1910 it was on the corner of Brewer Street, only a
fragment of which still survives. Next to the pub is Batson's
the florists, and a plumber's shop can be identified at number
62/63. The time on the Town Hall clock is 3.25 in the after-
noon. The Town Hall of the Metropolitan Borough of
Woolwich had been recently built when this photograph was
taken, as had the adjoining Hippodrome Theatre. Tall
chimneys, a sign of Woolwich's industrial prosperity, tower
in the background. The dome of Barclays Bank Chambers
remains unchanged.

*A strange anomalous mixture of the splendid and
the tame, the grand and the insignificant.*
Woolwich & its Environs 1837

Lower Wood Street, as it was called in 1910, with the famous Slazenger factory on the left. Slazengers came to Woolwich in the 1890s, and in 1902 their tennis balls started being used exclusively at the Wimbledon Championships. An associated local company, Gradidges, made cricket bats and golf clubs. Slazengers left the area in the 1940s and the building was taken over by the Stellex Ladder company.

Woolwich impresses as a happy place. Most of the older streets near the river and in the heart of the town are full of sturdy one-hundred-years-old houses, the tidy homes of a well-rooted race of working people.
London South of the River Sam Price Myers 1949

Woolwich from the river

From across the Thames Woolwich looks like a typical river-side town — a jumble of piers, wharves, taverns and houses. This picture can be dated sometime between 1905, when the Town Hall was built, and 1912 when the Foot Tunnel was opened (there is no sign in the photograph of construction having been started for the tunnel). The Steam Boat Pier is just distinguishable on the left next to Bell Watergate where the back of the *Crown and Cushion* public house can be seen. To the right is the free ferry pontoon. Right of Bell Watergate on the Borough Council's Wharf, is Wharf House whose 'Strawberry Hill Gothic' appearance contrasts sharply with the other riverside buildings. Only a few years after this photograph was taken the left-hand side of the view was startlingly changed by the addition of the Woolwich Power Station (started in 1912). The prominent buildings on the left are probably four tenement blocks which once stood at the top of Market Hill.

The old steam paddlers were magnets for East London boys who sometimes rode backwards and forwards for hours — or until they were chased off by the crews. The attraction was not so much the passing ships as the fascinating steam engines which could be watched from the ferries' alleyways.

The Spirit of London's River L M Bates 1980

Woolwich Ferry

. . . there is more wealth passes through Woolwich than any other place in the world.
Woolwich & Its Environs 1837

The Gordon

The Duncan

The Hutton

The Woolwich Free Ferry of 1889 and the Blackwall Tunnel of 1897 were designed to help Londoners living east of London Bridge who had no access to free bridges across the Thames, yet had to pay the same rates. An Act of 1885 gave the Metropolitan Board of Works (a forerunner of the LCC and GLC) power to run a ferry across the Thames at Woolwich. Two boats — the *Gordon* and the *Duncan* — provided the service when it was opened by Lord Rosebery, Chairman of the LCC, on 23 March 1889, and a third — the *Hutton* — was introduced in 1893. These three coke-fired paddle steamers maintained the service until the *Squires* was added in 1922

and a new *Gordon* a year later. Two new boats — the *John Benn* and the *Will Crooks* — joined the fleet in 1930.

In an effort to relieve the shopping streets of Woolwich from the congestion caused by traffic waiting for the ferries, new terminals and approach roads were planned during the 1960s. The new approach road, John Wilson Street, by-passed the busy shopping areas and in 1963 three new style diesel boats — the *Ernest Bevan,* the *John Burns* and the *James Newman* — were introduced to cope with the vastly increased lorry traffic. Rex Whitton, US Federal Highway Administrator, formally opened the new terminals in 1966.